Managing Children With ADHD:

Amazing guild on nurturing messes with ADHD kids as a novice.

Cheryl P. Olson

Table of contents

Chapter 1

What does ADHD mean for youngsters?

Messes around with ADHD frequently have conduct issues. They lash out rapidly, pitch fits, and decline to do things they would rather not do. These children aren't attempting to be awful. The issue is that ADHD can make it difficult for them to do things they view as troublesome or exhausting. It likewise makes them struggle with controlling themselves when they get baffled.

Messes around with ADHD are extremely inquisitive commonly. They can hardly hold back to see or do fascinating things, and they oppose exhausting or dreary things. This can be upsetting for guardians since it transforms things like schoolwork and sleeps time into fights. Messes with ADHD might contend or pitch fits to escape exhausting things. It tends to be enticing to give them their way, however that can instruct them that acting up works. All things considered, supportive pick-up nurturing procedures can assist messes around with working on their conduct over the long run.

Blowing your top typically doesn't help. If you holler a ton or rebuff them constantly, it will become typical and children will start to overlook it. All things being equal, messes with ADHD benefit from heaps of construction and applause when they do things right. To assist your kid with acting, tell them precisely what you would like them to do. Make sense of what conduct is OK and show them acceptable conduct so they can duplicate it. Acclaim them when they act well.

ADHD additionally makes it difficult for youngsters to control huge sentiments. They can lash out rapidly and experience difficulty with connections, therefore. Assisting messes around with ADHD frequently includes assisting them with figuring out how to quiet down when they blow up.

One of the most outstanding ways of assisting messes with ADHD and conduct issues is taking a parent instructional course. Guardians can figure out how to lessen struggle by utilizing acclaim and different devices to assist jokes around with controlling their way of behaving. Mental conduct treatment, interactive abilities preparing, and energizer drugs can likewise assist messes around with ADHD work on their way of behaving.

Fits and disobedience are not side effects of ADHD itself, but rather they are many times a consequence of ADHD side effects. Carelessness and impulsivity can make it truly challenging for youngsters to endure undertakings that are dull, or take a great deal of work, or children view as exhausting.

Kids with ADHD can be overpowered with dissatisfaction, and tossing a shoe or pushing somebody, or hollering "shut up!" can be the consequence of impulsivity. They are less capable than different children their age to oversee strong sentiments without an explosion.

Be that as it may, conduct issues can likewise go past indiscreet explosions. A few children with ADHD foster negative ways of behaving.

In situations where jokes with ADHD are persistently disobedient, they are likewise determined to have a conduct issue called oppositional rebellious turmoil (ODD). Upwards of 40% of children with ADHD are additionally analyzed withODD. Be that as it may, a lot greater amount of them are in the struggle with guardians or educators over their way of behaving — upwards of 80%, notices Dr. Anderson, a clinical clinician. Messes around with ADHD frequently have conduct issues. They lash out rapidly, pitch fits, and decline to do things they would rather not do. These children aren't attempting to be awful. The issue is that ADHD can make it difficult for them to do things they view as troublesome or exhausting. It likewise makes them struggle with controlling themselves when they get baffled.

Messes around with ADHD are extremely inquisitive commonly. They can hardly hold back to see or do fascinating things, and they oppose exhausting or dreary things. This can be upsetting for guardians since it transforms things like schoolwork and sleeps time into fights. Messes with ADHD might contend or pitch fits to escape exhausting things. It tends to be enticing to give them their way, however that can instruct them that acting up works. All things considered, supportive pick-up nurturing procedures can assist messes around with working on their conduct over the long run.

Blowing your top typically doesn't help. If you holler a ton or rebuff them constantly, it will become typical and children will start to overlook it. All things being equal, messes with ADHD benefit from heaps of construction and applause when they do things right.

To assist your kid with acting, tell them precisely what you would like them to do. Make sense of what conduct is OK and show them acceptable conduct so they can duplicate it. Acclaim them when they act well.

ADHD additionally makes it difficult for youngsters to control huge sentiments. They can lash out rapidly and experience difficulty with connections, therefore. Assisting messes around with ADHD frequently includes assisting them with figuring out how to quiet down when they blow up.

One of the most outstanding ways of assisting messes with ADHD and conduct issues is taking a parent instructional course. Guardians can figure out how to lessen struggle by utilizing acclaim and different devices to assist jokes around with controlling their way of behaving. Mental conduct treatment, interactive abilities preparing, and energizer drugs can likewise assist messes around with ADHD work on their way of behaving.

Fits and disobedience are not side effects of ADHD itself, but rather they are many times a consequence of ADHD side effects.

Carelessness and impulsivity can make it truly challenging for youngsters to endure undertakings that are dull, or take a great deal of work, or children view as exhausting.

Kids with ADHD can be overpowered with dissatisfaction, and tossing a shoe or pushing somebody, or hollering "shut up!" can be the consequence of impulsivity. They are less capable than different children their age to oversee strong sentiments without an explosion.

Be that as it may, conduct issues can likewise go past indiscreet explosions. A few children with ADHD foster negative ways of behaving.

In situations where jokes with ADHD are persistently disobedient, they are likewise determined to have a conduct issue called oppositional rebellious turmoil (ODD).

Chapter 2

Nurturing messes with ADHD kids as a novice

Nurturing is just about as significant as some other piece of ADHD treatment. The manner in which guardians answer can exacerbate ADHD.

Assuming your youngster has been determined to have ADHD:

Be involved. Realize all you can about ADHD. Follow the treatment your kid's medical services supplier suggests. Go to all suggested treatment visits. Assuming your youngster takes ADHD prescriptions, give them at the suggested time. Try not to change the portion without checking with your primary care physician. Keep your youngster's prescriptions in a protected spot where others can't get to them.

Know what ADHD means for your kid. Each kid is unique. Recognize the issues your kid has due to ADHD. A few children need to get better at focusing and tuning in. Others need to get better at dialing back. Ask your kid's advisor for tips and ways you can help your kid practice and get to the next level.

Center around showing your youngster each thing in turn. Try not to attempt to chip away at everything simultaneously. Begin little. Pick one thing to zero in on. Acclaim your youngster's work.
Work with your kid's school. Chat with your youngster's instructor to see whether your

kid ought to have an IEP or 504 arrangement. Meet frequently with instructors to figure out how your kid is doing. Work with the educator to assist your youngster with getting along admirably. Interface with others for help and mindfulness. Join a help association for ADHD like CHADD to seek refreshes on treatment and data, and so on.

See whether you have ADHD. ADHD frequently runs in families. Guardians (or different family members) of children with ADHD probably won't realize they have it as well. At the point when guardians with ADHD get analyzed and treated, it assists them with being at their best as guardians.

Discipline with reason and warmth. Realize what discipline approaches are best for a kid with ADHD and which can exacerbate ADHD. Get instructing from your youngster's specialist on ways of answering your kid's ways of behaving. Messes with ADHD may be delicate to analysis. Remedying their way of behaving is best finished in a manner that is empowering and strong as opposed to rebuffing.

Set clear assumptions. Before you head off to some place, talk with your kid to make sense of how you believe that they should act. Center more energy around training your youngster what to do, as opposed to responding to what not to do.

Discuss it. Try not to avoid consulting with your youngster about ADHD. Assist jokes around with understanding that having ADHD isn't their shortcoming and that they can learn ways of further developing the issues it causes.

Get to know one another consistently. Make time to talk and appreciate unwinding, fun exercises with your youngster — regardless of whether it's only for a couple of moments. Intently focus on your youngster. Praise positive ways of behaving. Try not to over-laud, yet remark when your kid accomplishes something great. For instance, when your youngster sits tight, say, "You're alternating so pleasantly."

Your relationship with your youngster makes the biggest difference. Messes with ADHD frequently feel they're letting others down, doing things wrong, or not being "great." Protect your youngster's confidence by showing restraint, understanding, and tolerating. Tell your kid you have faith in them and see every one of the beneficial things about them. Fabricate flexibility by keeping your relationship with your youngster positive and cherishing.

Chapter 3

Tips to Improve expertise to your ADHD kids.

Having ADHD can make a study hall experience hard for any youngster, particularly concerning tuning in. Fortunately, there are a few stages that guardians, children, and educators can take to assist understudies with ADHD in further developing their listening abilities and in general school insight. Here are our top tips to further develop listening abilities in messes with ADHD:

Have Students Clap Back a Pattern

While you will present another movement or give headings, begin by applauding an example to your understudies. Then, have them applaud it back to you. Rehash the example until each understudy is applauding the example back. This will guarantee that each understudy is fixed on what you're talking about and that they hear the bearings you're going to convey. At the point when understudies with ADHD can applaud back an example appropriately, it shows they are paying attention to the educator.

Mess around that Require Listening

Support listening abilities by messing around that require tuning in the homeroom. A few extraordinary instances of games that require understudies with

ADHD to listen to are Simon Says, Musical Chairs, and Mother May I.

Pose Inquiries Throughout Tasks

As your kid with ADHD is finishing responsibilities in the study hall or at home, ask them inquiries about the thing they're doing. You can get some information about the ongoing step they're finishing, or what they intend to handle straight away.

By having them converse with you about undertakings or make sense of what they're doing, you can guarantee they're centered around the main job and that they paid attention to their directions. This can not just urge them to listen more toward the beginning yet additionally guarantee that they remain on track all through.

Empower Note-Taking When Instructions are Being Given

If a youngster struggles with tuning in, urge them to take notes while being given directions, especially if they have questions. This will permit them to keep tuning in without interfering with the directions, and it will offer them the chance to forget about the inquiry for a brief time.

Then, at that point, offer all understudies the chance to pose the inquiries they've recorded later when every one of the guidelines has been given.

Chapter 4

Controlling ADHD normally

If you are a parent or overseer of a kid with ADHD, there are steps you can take to assist them with dealing with their condition and decrease dissatisfaction for everybody. Advance however much you can about ADHD. Work with their instructor and other school faculty to ensure they have the facilities they need to succeed. At home, center around:

Clear correspondence: Provide clear headings while speaking with them.

Association: Help your youngster stay coordinated by keeping their things in reliable spots.

Energy: Encourage and uphold your youngster in the areas where they show strength and assist them with perceiving their capacities in themselves.

Design and schedule: Stick to a customary timetable and make unsurprising schedules.

Rewards: Ensure they know while they're making the best choice. Acclaim them or deal with rewards.

Parent preparation might be a piece of conduct treatment for your kid if they are more youthful than 12 years of age. This preparation shows guardians abilities they can use to assist with working on a kid's way of behaving.